ACADEMY OF
LEARNING

Your Complete Preschool Lesson Plan Resource: Volume 1

© **2015 Breely, Crush & Associates, LLC**

Ver. 112014

Table of Contents

Educator Biography

Sharlit Elliott has a B.S. in Elementary Education and Early Childhood from Brigham Young University and has been a teacher for over 15 years working with children ages 3-5. She keeps current on changes in education by attending University classes and conferences several times a year. Besides having raised five children, she has held various leadership positions with the Girl Scouts and the 4-H program. She enjoys gardening, scrapbooking, reading and of course working with children.

How to Use This Book

This book is designed for a teacher working with children ages 3-5 in a classroom, homeschool or home preschool environment. One of the most important aspects of this series is that it includes fun activities that will enhance their skills. These lessons plans, games and ideas are all for you to use. Don't forget, these are complete lessons and activities that have been designed for compliance with federal and state guidelines for education. We go above and beyond to bring you MORE than what's expected in the public school system.

We will refer to your students as "your children or class". That includes whatever area you are using these lessons for: homeschool or preschool. Our lesson plans include improving student's abilities through activities. The skills we will be working with include: listening skills, music, movement, language and literacy, mathematics, science, fine motor, creative art, sensory, dramatic play, and social skills.

The book is organized by themes which will help you quickly find just the right information. The headings in the book will direct you quickly to large group, small group, and free time activities. It will also provide ideas for field trips.

This book will include the following areas:

Group Activities/Circle Time

- Music & Movement is used to help develop large muscles in arms and legs. These need to be developed before children can be successful in small muscles activities such as used in writing or cutting with scissors. This area also helps children learn to enjoy music and the basics such as beat, loud/soft and fast/slow.

- Language & Literacy is how we help children learn vocabulary, story order, thinking skills, recall, concepts of the theme, and expressive language.

Small Group Activities/Table Times

- Math & Cognitive is used to teach numbers, shapes, patterns, sorting, thinking and reasoning skills.

- Fine Motor Skills develop small muscles to be able to draw, write, manipulate small things, to tear, and to cut with scissors.

- Language & Literacy is used to develop skills such as expressive writing, visual memory, matching letters, letter sounds, categorizing items, directional words, and opposites.

- Other creative activities to develop their own uniqueness as an individual.

Free Time

- Creative arts to draw, build, and develop their imagination.

- Sensory activities are used to learn through exploration and using their senses.

- Dramatic Play & Social Development let children take on different roles, solve problems, find solutions, and develop social interactions.

- Science helps children explore by experimenting, identifying problems, guessing what will happen, checking to see what did happen, questioning how things happened, and developing a plan of what to do next.

- Gross Motor to practice using large and small muscles in fun activities.

- Field Trip Ideas to help children use real places to learn about the world.

Throughout the book we will use the following icons to show the different types of activities:

 MUSIC & MOVEMENT

 LANGUAGE & LITERACY

 MATH & COGNITIVE

 FINE MOTOR SKILLS

 CREATIVE ARTS

 SENSORY

 DRAMATIC PLAY & SOCIAL DEVELOPMENT

 SCIENCE

 GROSS MOTOR SKILLS

 FIELD TRIP IDEAS

Introduction Unit/First of the Year Set-up

This introduction unit provides you with helps to get you started and ideas that you can use through the year. There are many things that you will need to do in order to be prepared for the beginning of the year. Even homeschooling parents can benefit from many of the ideas of creating specific areas for activities and learning, helping to eliminate distractions and create a fun and positive environment.

NAME TAGS

Name tags serve the purpose of identification for adults who work with the children and also to help the children learn name recognition of their own name as well as other children's names.

Name tags can be a simple rectangle or oval shape out of construction paper and then laminated to make them more durable. They can also be in the shape of an apple or leaf for fall, a snowman or snowflake for winter, a tulip or butterfly for spring, or a sun or shell for summer.

You can also have these tags hard laminated at a copy store for increased durability. Don't forget to punch a hole in them before they are laminated if you are going to attach them with a large safety pin. Laminating can be done at an office supply store or a copy center. You can also attach them with a clip available from an office supply store instead of using a safety pin.

Another option is to buy place-mats and cut your shapes from them and use a permanent maker to write children's names on them. Place-mats can be found in the household section of your local department or discount store.

Make name tags for field trips as above, but do not put the children's names on them. Instead write the school's name and phone number on it. Example of tag: "Hi! I'm from Learning School. Please call my school 597-123-4567 if I'm lost or need help." The reason for not having the children's names on the tags is to keep strangers from knowing children's names. Without this information, they will not be able to call to them by using their name. The school number listed on the tag is in case a child ever becomes separated from the group, an adult finding a child will be able to help the child get back to where he/she belongs.

CIRCLE TIME

What is circle time? Circle time is when the children sit on the floor for large group instruction. During this time they will sing songs, do movement activities, have story time or other literacy experiences all together. You can make places for the children to sit—and it can be as simple as shapes cut and laminated (as shown) and then use clear wide tape, to tape them to the floor. The shape I prefer is a semicircle facing the teacher.

Another idea is to buy placemats and either a plain colored one or turn pattern ones over to the plain side. Next, cut the mats down the middle and write each child's name on a mat. Then on the first day of school have the children draw a picture of whatever they want on their mat using permanent markers and attach a piece of Velcro (the raised nib side) on the bottom of their mats so that they will stick to the rug. This way the mats can be moved for cleaning the rug and changing seating assignments easily. Before you put them down cover the children's drawings with clear contact paper to keep the colors from coming off and to keep them clean.

A Child Placemat

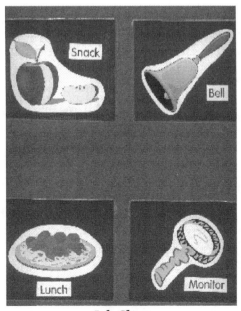

Job Chart

JOB CHARTS

Job charts help children be responsible and feel good about themselves. There are many different ways to do this. One way is to have a can labeled with the each of the class jobs. Some examples of jobs you might choose could be: plant care, pet care, door holder, monitor, song leader, line leader, children counter, and snack helper.

Follow these steps to make your own job chart:

1. First trace the children's hands and write their names on hands.

2. Next attach hands to a Popsicle stick.

3. Place the children's hand names into the various cans with the hand facing out.

4. Then take turns drawing hands out of a zip-lock bag that has all the children's names inside it. The person drawn out is that particular helper for the day. These helpers can be placed in a pocket for all to see or stick into the top of a box. For the box use an empty shoe box or any small box and cover it with bright paper.

5. Next cut slits in the top of the box, one for each job. You can vary containers or use a circle instead of the hand and have children draw their own face on the circle.

Another idea is to make a poster with pockets taped on it and different jobs on or under each pocket. Then pick from the hands or face shapes job helpers and place that child's shape in the desired pocket. You can have children keep the same job all week or you can change jobs daily, whatever works best for you and your class. Job charts are also good for children doing homeschool. Building self-esteem is good for all children. Find an easy to complete household job for them to complete or modify other school related tasks.

CHILD'S CUBBIES (LOCKER)

The cubbies should have the children's names and a picture of themselves to help them learn where to put their things and to recognize their name. You can write their names by hand or on the computer and laminate them for durability. Print names using both upper and lower case letters and include first and last names. I use the poster putty to hold them to their locker.

Take pictures of each child when they register for school or on the first day of class. Children can make a frame for their pictures by gluing tongue depressors sticks (or Popsicle sticks) into a square shape. Then after they are dry, they can collage on the frame using one of the following: foam shapes, colored macaroni, sequins or old small puzzle pieces. These frames with their pictures can now be placed with poster adhesive (the white putty like material that can be used to hang posters, etc., without leaving holes in the wall) locker near their names. Also, provide a large zip lock bag with each child's name on it for the parents to put a change of clothing inside to keep at school in case of an accident. These bags will be kept inside their cubbies.

DAILY SCHEDULE

A daily schedule should be posted for parents to read and a poster with a pictures schedule for the children to follow. This poster can show last year's class or drawings of children doing the various activities. Examples: children sitting in a circle singing, children washing their hands for snack, children eating snack, children going to small groups—working on things at the table, children playing at sensory table, children painting at easel, children playing house, children at circle doing a movement activity, children taking their work and lining up to go home. This will help children feel comfortable about what they will be doing and when they will be able to go home. This also helps children that do not speak English know what is happening.

NAMES

Names of the children can be used in so many ways during the year, so write them or print them and laminate them. They can use them to trace their names if written large. Use a light weight paper and place it over their name to trace.

They can use the name slips on a poster or chalk board to vote for something. Example: Do you like apples or oranges? Divide columns into apples and oranges with the picture of the fruit above and spaces below for name slips for voting. Children take turns voting by placing (using tape or plastic putty) their name under which fruit they like. Next when all the children have voted, have the children count the number of names under each picture to see which fruit is like more or which is liked less.

They can also use their name slips to look at while practicing writing their names with markers or pencils or writing their names with shaving cream.

You can also add a picture of each child to a poster with their names below so they can learn each other's names. Then they can write the other children's names and draw a picture to give them. They will learn to recognize many of the other children's names and begin to learn letter names.

Getting to Know You

MUSIC & MOVEMENT

1. Sing the song **"Hickety Pickety Bumblebee"** Children take turns singing their name and they learn each others names while singing this song. The second time you sing this song as a group, have the children whisper their name and the third time you sing the song, have the children clap the syllables in their name.

> Hickety Pickety Bumblebee,
>
> Can you sing your name to me? (Child says name)
>
> Hickety Pickety Bumble Bee.
>
> Can you whisper your name for me? (whisper child's name)
>
> Hickety Pickety Bumble Bee,
>
> Can you clap your name for me?
>
> (clap syllables).

2. Another great song to sing is the **"Plate Name Song"**.

    "Plate Name Song" (Tune: If You're Happy and You Know It)

> If your name is on the plate pick it up.
>
> If your name is on the plate pick it up.
>
> If your name is on the plate,
>
> Then you're really doing great.
>
> If your name is on the plate pick it up.

Write each child's name on a plastic or disposable plate. Sing the song in a circle, putting a child's plate in the middle for each verse. Whichever child's name is on the plate has to pick up that plate. Keep singing until all of the plates are gone.

3. **"One Little Apple"**—Teacher walks around circle of children while singing song with an apple. Teacher stops near one child and pretends to drop apple on child's head while continuing to sing song. Teacher keeps doing this until all of the children have had the apple dropped on their head and teacher has said their name.

4. Sing the song **"Five Little Monkeys Jumping on The Bed"** with the finger play actions.

5. Sing the song **"Where is Thumbkin?"**

6. Sing the song **"One Little Elephant"**—Make small elephant heads and put a hole where the elephant's trunk would be. Laminate heads so they will be durable. Children place their littlest finger through the hole to be the elephant's trunk while singing this song.

 ## LANGUAGE & LITERACY

Take the children on a tour of your classroom and show them the different areas such as the bathroom, the sink, the books, the creative art supplies, the sensory table, puzzles, math table, writing table, and the dramatic play things. Talk about a few simple rules that you have in each area as you show them.

Back at the circle have the children help you think of rules for the classroom. Write and draw the simple rules that the children suggest. Post these rules to remind and refer back to as needed. Example of a rule, "We will have kind hands". Use a picture of a hand with the writing to help the children remember.

Use a poster made earlier that shows the class the schedule through drawings or photos. Go through the schedule with them. Talk with them about the various activities on the poster that you will do and when they will be going back home. This helps the children feel more confident about the day, they know what will be happening and when they will see their parents again. Talk the children about the signal you have decided on to let them know that it is time for them to clean up the room and come back to the circle. This signal could be a song, a bell, or drum rhythm on a drum.

Concept—review class rules and talk about what it would be like if the class had no rules. Act out using hand puppets some of the class rules. These are some books that you might like to read to the group:

<u>Brown Bear, Brown Bear, What Do You See</u> by Bill Martin Jr./Eric Carle, Henry Holt & Company, 1992.

<u>The Kissing Hand</u> by Audrey Penn, Scholastic Inc., 1993.

<u>Huddly Goes to School</u> by Tedd Arnold Scholastic Inc., 2000.

After reading a story or two, transition the group to table time and small group activities.

 ## MATH & COGNITIVE

Use small plastic boxes to house things for the children to explore. These plastic boxes can have various small items inside them, such as old buttons and keys, lots of different small shaped erasers and small colored wood shapes. You can buy many different small items at discount stores like Partyland, Dollar Stores or Oriental Trading. Children choose their own box and empty it out. Next they could play with the items inside and spend some time exploring them. Later they could separate items by color, shape or size. They put the items back into their box before getting another one or before leaving the table.

Children enjoy puzzles on another day, but be sure and have some wood ones with handles and few pieces for beginners along with others puzzles with up to 12 pieces in them for more advanced children.

Put out paper and plastic boxes of different sizes with lids, also put out jars of various sizes with lids and have the children match the lids to the containers.

FINE MOTOR SKILLS

Children will glue collage items on a tongue depressor picture frame. (see Child's cubbies at the beginning of this section).

Have play dough made to set out along with rolling pins, different cookie cutter shapes and garlic presses to use with the dough.

Also set out manipulatives such as Lego's Duplo (large plastic building blocks) or Space Links for children to use.

Provide wood blocks for children to create buildings and other structures.

LANGUAGE & LITERACY

Put out place mats for each child with their names on them (see circle time above). Children will use permanent markers to decorate them. Children will dictate to teacher something about their drawing. Teacher will add the words on mats based on what the children tell about the objects drawn on their mat.

Prepare a tape or CD with different sounds on it such as the toilet flushing, a hammer pounding, a bell ringing and the clean-up song for the children to identify. Teacher will also have drawings or photos of the objects for the children to see. Children will take turns identifying the sound made and holding up the picture of the object used to make the sound.

For another activity, the teacher will prepare two sets of photos of the same item. These pictures will be of things that children do at school such as sitting at circle time and eating snack. The teacher will use one set of photos for this first activity. Children will take turns picking a card to show to the other children. Then the child will tell what he/she thinks is happening in the picture. Next the next the teacher will help the children arrange the cards on the table in the correct order of what they do each day.

Another day the children will use both sets of photos. They will take turns drawing a card and then finding its match. They will say what is happening in the picture and the next child will take their turn. The play continues until all the cards have been matched. Next they will arrange the photos in correct order as they did the first day.

CREATIVE ARTS

Set up an easel with poster paint, paper and aprons to keep their clothes clean.

SENSORY

Set up a sensory table. Sensory tables encourage children to learn about their environment through their sense of touch. Use an official sensory table that has places for water or sand built in, or you can use what you have on hand by simply setting a plastic tub on top of the table. The advantage to having the tubs built in is that the children are much less likely to accidentally spill an entire table of water or sand compared to a bucket or bin. For this activity, use water in the table with rubber ducks, small nets and plastic baskets to hold the scooped up ducks. The Teacher should encourage children to count the ducks captured and then put them in baskets.

DRAMATIC PLAY & SOCIAL DEVELOPMENT

For this area of development you will need to set up a part of the classroom for dramatic play. This is basically an area where the children can play "house" or "dress-up". Although it may seem that we do this activity simply because the children enjoy it, they are actually learning how to deal in different social situations, solve problems, etc. Some ideas for having in the area include: men and women clothing, shoes, hats, wallets and purses, along with child sized kitchen appliances, tables and chairs. Children also enjoy having dolls and doll clothing to use in pretending.

SCIENCE

Science time allows children to learn about their environment through experiments and help teach them to love learning. For this introduction week/lesson, furnish this station with on sunflowers, a sunflower with seeds in it to examine, magnifying glasses, and shelled seeds to taste.

GROSS MOTOR

Children will play "Red Light, Green Light" outside. The teacher will have two paper plates. One will have a large green circle inside it and the other will have a large red circle inside it. Teacher will ask children to tell the colors of the circles and teacher will explain green it for go and red is for stop. The children will stand at one end and the teacher will stand at the other end of a large space either inside or outside. When teacher shows the plates with the color green the children must run, hop, or skip (depending on teacher instructions) to touch her/him when it's red they must stop. Teacher will alternate between colors. The child that touches the teacher first is when "it" and takes the teachers place. The children go back to the other side and the game begins again with the teacher helping the "it" child.

Colors

GROUP ACTIVITIES/CIRCLE TIME

   MUSIC & MOVEMENT

"Brown Bear, Brown Bear What Do You See?" by Bill Martin Jr./Eric Carle, Henry Holt & Company, 1992. (Show pictures in the book while you sing the song or make your own animal pictures to use with the song.)

"I'm Scat the Cat" (Draw picture of cat on clear sheet protector and put different colors of paper inside so when you change colors of cat you can remove a page and the cat will change colors.

"Color Hoedown" by Marilyn LaPenta, Macmillan Book Clubs, Inc., 1989. Song "Color Hoedown will have the children dancing with the instruction on the tape.

"My Favorite Color" by Heather Forest, Macmillan Book Clubs, Inc., 1989. Children will review colors of different items in this song.

   LANGUAGE & LITERACY

Children will hunt in the room to match color signs to colors shown them. They will bring color signs back to circle and say color names with help if needed. Children enjoy hearing the following books about colors:

The Color Kittens by Margaret Wise Brown, Western Publishing Company, Inc., 1994.

Seven Blind Mice by Ed Young, Scholastic Inc., 1992.

My Many Colored Days by Dr. Seuss, Scholastic Inc., 1997.

Cat's Colors by Jane Cabrera, Scholastic Inc., 1998.

Concept—review color names showing color signs and saying color names. Put shaving cream in a zip-lock bag with a little food coloring. Ask the children what they think will happen next. Pass the bag around and have the children squeeze it carefully and then talk about the color. Repeat this activity with different colors. On another day or later in the lesson, put two different colors in the bag with the shaving cream. Ask the children what color that they think it will be when mixed together. Record what color they guess it will be by having small papers for each child and crayons available for them. The children will choose a crayon the color that they think the new color will be and make a dot or other mark on their page to record their answer. Use the three primary colors (red, yellow & blue) in different combinations for this activity. You may want to do different combinations of primary colors on different days. Discuss what happened when you mixed the colors and have them record what color it really made on their papers next to their guesses. Children will compare the two colors to see if they guessed correctly. Ask if they think mixing other things that are colored will work the same way. Then give them opportunities at table time to find out.

SMALL GROUP ACTIVITIES/TABLE TIMES

 ## MATH & COGNITIVE

Children will sort small toys such as bears by color and then count the toys in each color with the help of teacher. Another day have the children match colored pom poms to felt colored circles placed inside of muffin tins and say their color names.

Next cut white paper into 3 inch by 11 inch strips and glue 2 inch squares in two different colors on the strips using a different pattern on each stripes. You may choose to alternate the two colors. (example—red, yellow, red, yellow, red) or make the stripes in more colors. Give a different strip to each child at the table to use. You may want to laminate the strips that they are copying, so they can be used again. Then provide a set of colored squares for the child to place on their cards. Talk about the fact that they made a pattern. Have children exchange cards and make a pattern again being mindful that the squares go from left to right in their placement and not in a random match. The last day give each child a slip of white paper and two colors of squares and have them glue their squares on the slip of paper to make a two color pattern without the aid of the patters slips.

You can also have the children sort building blocks by color or size. You could go on a color hunt around the room for different colors.

Create your own color matching game with a muffin tin. Glue colored paper or buttons into the bottom. Have the children practice matching the colors and putting them in the correct hole.

FINE MOTOR SKILLS

Children will each be given a small ball of two different primary colors of play dough. They will squeeze the two balls together until they are mixed and make a new color. Then the next day put all the same colors of dough together and let the children play with the dough, keeping the same colors together not mixed. Provide rolling pins and cookie cutters to use with the dough. Another day have children tear different colors of construction paper and talk about the colors that they have torn. Next have them glue their strips on a plain piece of paper to make their own design. The last day provide children with aprons, shaving cream and shakers of powdered tempera (poster paint). Squirt some shaving cream on the table in front of each child and let them figure paint in it. As the children tire of this let them shake a small amount of the powdered tempera onto their shaving cream to color it. Talk about the new color. You can find powdered tempera at a school supple store or an office supple store such as Staples. You can duplicate this activity by using Ziploc bags and tempera paint. Squeeze in yellow and red, then let the children mix the bag until the colors mix.

You can also have children hunt for colors in magazines and cut them out to post on a color page. Or divide the page into different sections with a color assigned to each section.

LANGUAGE & LITERACY

Tell the children that they will be playing a game with you. She will have index cards with different colors on each card. Children will take turns drawing a card from the pile and all the children will say the color name together. Next the child that drew the card will find something in the room that is the same color and point it out to the other children. The next child will draw a card and find something the same color as before. The game continues until all the color cards have been matched to a color in the room.

Teacher will read the book <u>Brown Bear, Brown Bear What Do You See,</u> by Bill Martin Jr./Eric Carle, Henry Holt & Company, 1992 and the children will all say the color and the animal name for each page of the store.

The teacher will provide a color match game by making one or buying one. To make one, use white index cards and draw a simple shape for each card such as a heart. Color two hearts the same color and keep working until you have two of each colors that you want the children to learn the color names. To play the game turn the cards face down and have the children take turns drawing three cards to try and make one match. If they make a match the child says the color name of the match and puts that match in front of him/her. The next child draws three cards if they don't make a match, they have to put their cards back down on the table face down and it's the next child's turn. Play continues until all of the cards have been matched and their color names have been said.

Teacher will read the book <u>My Crayons Talk</u> by Patricia Hubbard, Scholastic Inc., 1997.

Next discuss with the children how different colors make them feel and give them a piece of paper and crayons to draw their own page with colors they like. Children will dictate to the teacher something about how their colors made them feel. The teacher will put all the class pictures together to make a book for their library.

FREE TIME

 CREATIVE ARTS

Creative Arts—the easel will be sat up with two primary colors on each side of the easel. Children will be able to experiment with the paint and see if they can make new colors on their paper at the easel. Use aprons for protection of their clothes and a place for drying the wet paintings.

SENSORY

Sensory—have sand in the sensory table or use pails as a sensory table with small colored objects, such as different colored erasers buried in the sand for the children to find. Also have an empty egg carton or muffin tin with different colors marked in the bottom of each section. When the children find the items buried they will place them in the matching space of the egg carton of muffin tin.

DRAMATIC PLAY & SOCIAL DEVELOPMENT

Dramatic Play & Social Development—set up a paint store. Use paint stripes colors from your local paint store so customers can choose their paint colors. Get old wallpaper books too. Have a toy cash register, play money, purses, wallets, paint caps, chip boards with paper and pencils, sacks, and empty paint cans (ice cream buckets) with paint brushes. Then provide a time for them to go outside to paint the sidewalks with their pretend paint (water) in their buckets or provide large boxes to paint with poster paint and brushes.

SCIENCE

Science—Children will have color paddles to look through in the primary colors. They will also have flashlights to use to shine through the color paddles. They will discover that light can also mix to make new colors. If you do not have color paddles use empty paper towel rolls with different colored cellophane over the one end and fasten with elastic. Children look through them like a spy glass. You can find the paper in craft supply stores or at Easter time most stores will carry it to put over the baskets.

GROSS MOTOR

Teacher will provide a large appliance box for the children to paint with poster paint. They will use small regular paint brushes and small pails of poster paint. They can make it into a store, a house or whatever they want. The teacher could cut out window for the children if they wanted them and assist them as needed.

FIELD TRIP IDEAS

Visit a paint store and watch how they mix the paint. Also ask them to give you a demonstration on painting and or wallpapering. Prepare the children before the trip by talking about what they will see and encourage them to come up with what they would like to see and learn while there. Make up a lotto card of things that you want them to find while there. Each child will receive a copy of the pictures of the items that you want the children to look for while at the store. They will also have a crayon to mark the things that they find. They will keep looking with their group until all of the items have been found. Assign teachers and parents to be with a small group of children. Talk about field trip rules and have everyone wear a special field trip name tag. (See first of year information for name tags.) The next day at school review what you learned and have the children make individual pictures to thank the store. The children will dictate the words to the teacher during small groups language and literacy time. Then be sure to take the pictures into the store to thank them.

Shapes

GROUP ACTIVITIES/CIRCLE TIME

 MUSIC & MOVEMENT

Sing "One Blue Square" and "Circle" found in Piggyback Songs Warren Publishing House, 1983. Make shape of square and circle with pointing finger while singing songs. Introduce only one shape a day. Another song to sing with the tape is "Artie the Octagon" by John Given, Macmillan Book Clubs, Inc. 1989.

Other shape songs can be made to go with tunes you already know such as—tune "Hi-Ho-the Dairy -O". Example:

Triangle Song

A triangle is like a roof

A triangle is like a roof

It has three sides

They go up down

And over an back

A triangle is like a roof.

Have the children trace the shapes in the air while singing songs.

Also make a large book with different shapes on each page and sing "I See Many Shapes" to the tune of "Brown Bear" which is also "Twinkle Twinkle Little Star".

Circle, Circle

What do you see?

I see a square looking at me.   *Turn the page of the book*

Square, Square

What do you see?

I see a rectangle looking at me.   *Turn the page of the book*

Rectangle, Rectangle

What do you see?

I see an Oval looking at me   *Turn the page of the book*

Continue adding shapes to the song until you have included all shapes that you wanted in song. On the last page do shape names and ask again what do you see? Turn the page and sing I see many shapes looking at me. Point to each small shape on that page and sing—We see a square (name of shape that is pointed) looking at me. Continue singing until all shapes have been reviewed.

 LANGUAGE & LITERACY

Read books on shapes:

There's a Square by Mary Sterfoz, Scholastic Inc., 1996.

Big Bird's Square Meal, by Emily Thompson, Western Publishing Company, Inc., 1988.

Active Minds Shapes by George Siede and Donna Preis,

After reading the books ask questions such as "What is your favorite shape?" and "Tell me something you remember about the story."

Each day have the children find the shape of the day in the classroom. Example: children look around the classroom and discover square windows, square tiles on the floor and square pictures on the walls.

Concept—Children will learn and review basic shapes. Use a can, a box or a bag to put shape objects into. Next have the children take turns putting their hand into the container and feeling a shape and then naming it. Another activity to do is have three or four shapes shown to the children. Then take one shape away while the children have their eyes closed. Next have them open their eyes and take turns guessing which shape is missing.

Another day, hide different shapes in a certain area of the room or outside and have the children find them. Then assemble the children together and have them name their shapes. Next have the children group all the same shapes together and count each shape type.

SMALL GROUP ACTIVITIES/TABLE TIMES

MATH & COGNITIVE

This week children will each make their own shape book for the song "I See Many Shapes". (See above Music and Movement) Write the words for each page for the children's books by hand or print words on computer for each page. Also make cover by putting title of book and write "by" with a place for children to write their own names. During the week children will do various projects to put the shapes on the correct pages and when all of the pages have been completed place all the pages inside the cover to form a book. They can take home their book to practice learning their shapes. The following are math shape pages and other shape pages will be included under the fine motor activities.

Make various sizes of circles that will fit on your shape page out of colored construction paper. You can punch out circles with paper punches or trace around circle items (example—lid from glue stick). Children will glue them on their circle page by ordering them from smallest to largest.

On another day, punch out rectangles or trace and cut out rectangles. Write the number 1-5 on each rectangle. Children will glue them on the rectangle page for their book in correct order 1-5.

Other ideas to do this week: have coins taped to the back of octagons and diamonds have the children match the same coins together and then say the name of the coin and corresponding shape. (Example—penny, diamond)

Use stickers of various shapes or punches make patterns. These shapes will be glued onto a strip of paper long enough to go around children's heads and about 2 to 2 ½ inches wide, for a each child to have their own headband.

 FINE MOTOR SKILLS

Use these ideas to complete your I See Many Shapes book:

Trace or print an oval on to your page with the correct words on the page, "Oval". Children trace the oval lines with glue and then sprinkle glitter over the glue and dump off the excess glitter in a large box lid.

Trace on poster board, triangles to fit on their triangle pages and cut a few for the children to use. Children will place the triangles on colored paper and trace around the edges and cut them out with scissors. Next they will glue their cut out triangle onto their triangle page.

Print a square or use a ruler to draw a square that will fit your shape pages. Have children use glue to put beans, rice or other small items on the outside lines of the square shape.

Print or trace a heart that will fit on your shape page. Children will use markers to create a design inside the heart shape.

Print or trace a diamond that will fit your diamond shape page. Children will use watercolors to paint the inside of the diamond for their book. Trace several stars on sandpaper and cut them out. Children will use the sandpaper shape on the page for stars. Have them use a crayon to rub back and forth across the top of the paper over the sandpaper until all the star has appeared on their page as a rubbing. Any of these ideas can be adjusted. The basic idea is to create the I See Many Shapes book and for the children to learn the shapes from working with them.

26

Another activity that you can do is tracing shapes. Before class, create large shapes on laminated paper. Give the children shoelaces or yarn to copy the shape with. They can place the string on top of your drawn copy.

LANGUAGE & LITERACY

Children will play shape bingo as a class. You can purchase the game at a school supply store or make your own cards by drawing lines on papers and adding basic shapes in the squares. Use index cards to draw large shapes on to represent each shape used on bingo cards. These cards will be your calling cards.

Draw them from the stack and show them one at a time to the children, they will name the shape and tell its color. Next they will look for a match on their bingo cards and place a maker such as a button, bean or penny on top of the matching shape. Make the shapes different colors so that you will not need so many different shapes. For example, have three triangles, a red one, a yellow one and a green one. Children will have to match shape color as well as shape to put a marker on it. The object of the game is to help children learn shape names and review color names. Children will continue with the game until they have filled their card or get four in a straight line.

Another game they will like to play again and again is memory match. Use index cards and cut them in half. On one side draw a matching shape on two cards. For example, draw a green triangle on each card, the second card is the match. Make sure that you use a scrapbook pen or marker that will not show through the paper.

After you have made seven matching sets you are ready to have the children play. Place the seven matching sets of shapes face down in a mixed up order. Have the children turn over two cards and try a get matching cards. The children will show their cards and tell the shape names. If the cards match, they may continue to draw two more cards until they no longer have matching cards. Next, the player will turn the cards back face down for the next player. Then the next player turns over two cards trying to recall where the cards that did not match were, so that they can find matching cards. Play continues until all the cards have been matched.

FREE TIME

CREATIVE ARTS

Cut out large paper shapes for the easel. The children will use "bingo marker" (they type of marker used in bingo tournaments. They create a circle of ink on the card) to create their own dot pattern inside the shapes. You can obtain bingo markers at Dollar stores or party shops.

SENSORY

Put wood shavings inside the sensory table with plastic magnetic shapes hidden in them. Children will find the shapes using fishing poles. They will say the shape name and place them in a small basket. When all magnetic shapes have been found, children will count the number in their basket and dump them back in the wood shavings. Make the fishing pole by using a dowel stick with a piece of yarn tied around it and yarn handing down about 15 inches. At the other end tie a round magnet with a hole in the center. Magnets and dowel rods/sticks can be found in any hardware store.

DRAMATIC PLAY & SOCIAL DEVELOPMENT

Children will use empty cereal boxes, egg carton, milk jugs, salt containers, frozen vegetable carton and other varies items to use for a pretend grocery store. They will also use sacks and cash registers with pretend money. Children will learn to share and take turns while using the materials.

SCIENCE

Use an empty number ten sized, coffee can or similar can to make a feely can. A feely can is a way to use touch and their imagination in order for figure out what is inside.

Wash it out and dry it. Then use a large size men's sock. Cut the cuff part off and use this part to glue to the inside of the can at the top of the can, so that the cuff sticks out from the can. Use craft glue for this. When it is dry, you can put plastic shapes inside the can and the children will not be able to see the shapes. They will have to feel the shapes with their hand and determine what shape they have found. Next they pull it out through the opening and see if they are correct. The science table or class room should also have something live on it to watch, such as a fish bowl with fish and or a green plant.

GROSS MOTOR

Make a card for each child that has basic shapes on them. Then take pictures of each shape and tape them to the floor. Have the children take turns throwing a beanbag at the shapes on the floor. When they hit a particular shape, they say its name and mark off the shape on their card with a check or line. They continue to toss the bag until they have marked off all the shapes on their card.

You can also make shapes on the floor with masking tape. Have the children walk around the group of shapes, naming them as they pass. You can duplicate this outside by using sidewalk chalk.

FIELD TRIP IDEAS

When riding in the bus or their car while coming and going to school have them look for shapes such as the rectangle shape of windows and have them name the shapes they see to others.

Go for a walk around the neighborhood and have them notice the shapes in everyday objects. You can tie in any activity that you want, showing the shape of an ice cream cone, otter pop, orange, etc.

Transportation

GROUP ACTIVITIES/CIRCLE TIME

 MUSIC & MOVEMENT

Teacher sings the, "The Wheels on the Bus".

> The wheels on the bus go round and round,
>
> Round and round, round and round,
>
> The wheels on the bus go round and round,
>
> All through the town.

Children act out the song such as going up and down from their seats for first verse, pretending to open shut doors and etc. "Wheels on the Bus" from "Raffi Rise and Shine", Homeland Publishing, Rounder Records Corp. tape & CD.

Also use "Row, Row, Row" from the same tape "Raffi Rise and Shine".

"Down By the Station" and "Sailing At High Tide are two other fun songs to use that are from the book, <u>Eye Winker Tom Tinker Chin Chopper</u> by Tom Glazer, Doubleday & Company, 1973.

Another fun song to sing is "Little Red Caboose."

> Little red caboose chug, chug, chug
>
> Little red caboose chug, chug, chug
>
> Little red caboose behind the train, train, train
>
> Smokestack on its back, back, back, back
>
> Coming down the track, track, track, track
>
> Little red caboose behind the train.
>
> Oooh, Oooh.

Teacher is the engine (1st in line). She sings the song while moving (her/his) arms in a circle position like wheels. She stops at the end of the song in front of a child or group of children and they get behind the teacher. The song and movement continues and at the end of the song, as before, the teacher stands in front of another child or group of children. They join behind the other children and become the caboose. They continue singing and moving their arms while they go to the next child or children. This procedure continues until all the children have joined the train.

 LANGUAGE & LITERACY

Choose how many days you will be talking about transportation and divide categories into that number of days and the amount of details you want to include. If the children are really interested continue on the next day adding more details to that category. For example, read books about things that go on the ground, in the air, or in the water. These are a few good books that you could read in different categories:

Truck Talk by Bobbi Katz Published by Scholastic Inc., 1997.

The Little Engine That Could retold by Watty Piper, Price/Stern/Sloan Publishers, Inc., 1986.

I've Been Working on the Railroad Nadine Bernard Westcott, Published by Scholastics Inc., 1997.

Freight Train by Donald Crews, Published by Scholastics Inc., 1989.

Sail Away by Donald Crews, Published by Scholastic Inc., 1995.

Cars! Cars! Cars! By Grace Maccarone, Scholastic Inc., 2000.

The Airplane Book by Edith Kunhardt, Western Publishing Company, Inc., 1987.

Going Places Western Publishing Company, Inc., 1988.

Concept—after reading each type of book on the different days get into the details that you want the children to know about. Ask questions such as, "What color was the caboose in the Freight Train?" Next ask, "What do you think could be in the tank car?" Why do you think it has liquids inside it? What could the liquids be? Continue on asking about each car in the story and its color. Also talk about how the train looked when going slow and fast and then how it looked in darkness and daylight. You could count the cars and talk about the order on them. Ask what is the name of the first part of the train (engine) and the last part (caboose)?

Read other books about trains with more details or fun ones that tell what the workers do like, I've Been Working on the Railroad. You could ask questions about what the workers on the train do and how they help others.

For an added social skill helper read The Little Engine That Could. Talk about what would have happened if the little train had not received help and how some of the other trains acted when they were asked to help. Relate it to the children in the class and how we need to help each other.

SMALL GROUP ACTIVITIES/TABLE TIMES

 ## MATH & COGNITIVE

Use tiny plastic train engines in two or more colors or punch out shapes of engines of different colors to write numbers on.

Write one number on each shape using numbers one through ten. Use set one through five until children learn six through ten numbers. Make several sets of these for children to use at the table.

Now we'll make a counting sheet/strip for each child to help in learning.

Make a 3 inch wide by 15 inches long strip on poster board for each set. Divide it with a marker into five boxes. Write numbers one through five at top of each square and put coordinating dots in each square. Have children match their engine number to the correct number square and say the number with you. If they do not recognize the number, have them count the dots. Then match the number toy to the square and say the number that they counted.

You can make the other side of the strip with the numbers six through ten for later use. Another activity for different day would be to use the same plastic items and make a color pattern with them. Example—red engine, blue engine, yellow engine, red engine, blue engine, yellow engine. If they need help making a pattern, make one for them and then let them copy yours just below it. Make sure that you tell them to make it in the same order as you do yours, so that they are not just matching. Patterning is an important skill used in many math skills.

When doing things that go in the air, use four toy airplanes of different sizes or drawings of four airplanes. You can draw one picture or find one in a book and use the copy machine to change the sizes. It is best to make them a lot bigger or smaller from each other, so they can tell the difference in them. Make several sets for the number of children that will be working with you at the table. Then take turns bring new children over to play with you until all the children have had a turn.

While the children are working with you have them arrange the items from smallest to largest or the other way around. If they need help have them find the largest and the smallest first, then have them compare the two remaining ones and ask which is the largest. Help them put it in between the largest and smallest. Next have them try to figure where the last one should go. If they still do not see where it goes, help them and say this is the next largest. It goes here.

On the water day, show the children how to make foil boats. Give each child a piece of foil about 12 inches long and have them bend and fold it to create their own boat. These boats do not have to look the same and should be made by them however they would like them. Next have a dishpan of water or use the sensory table with water to float the boats one at a time. Give the first child a container of marbles and have them place a marble one at a time of his/her boat as he/she counts. The child continues to add one marble at a time while continuing to count until the boat sinks. If the number of marbles is greater than the child can count help them to complete the task until it sink

You can also have all the children count with the child that is placing the marbles in their boat. Continue until all the children have had a turn. They are learning to count and also they are learning science skills you may wish to talk about: which boat held the most marbles, which shape held the most and what did they think was the best way to build their boat to hold the most marbles. You could give them another piece of foil the next day and talk about what happened in more detail.

FINE MOTOR SKILLS

Trains

Have children trace a train engine and some cars on a white piece of paper horizontal. Then have them draw the background trees of etc. The engine and cars should be cut out of heavy poster board.

Airplanes

Children can use tongue depressor sticks and/ or Popsicle sticks with wood glue to create their own airplane.

Cars/Trucks

Use a large car shape to cut watercolor paper for the children to paint in the details of a car.

Boats

Prepare an outline of a simple boat for each child via photo copying. Children will use colored glue to decorate the boat. You can color white glue with food coloring and bio-color. Bio-color comes in many colors and it can be used to color noodles too. It is available through school supply stores.

LANGUAGE & LITERACY

Tell the story of Albert the Auto which is as follows:

Albert Auto was a happy little car until one day he noticed that all the cars on the road were shiny and had no dents. He noticed that he had a few dents and that his paint was coming off. He was sad about how he looked and he began to cry.

Bluebird flew over where Albert was crying and he asked him why he was sad. Albert told him that he did not look good anymore with dents and his paint peeling off. Bluebird knew how kind that Albert was and told him that he was his friend and that he wanted to help him. Bluebird said that he had a Woodpecker friend that could peck all his dents out. This made Albert happy, but he still worried about his paint.

The woodpecker did come and he was happy to help Albert remove all the dents. Albert had been thinking how nice his friend, Bluebird, had been to help and how even the Woodpecker had helped him. He decided that he needed to help others too. So, the very next day when he saw Woodpecker he asked what he could do to help him. Woodpecker said that he needed a place to sleep and Albert told him that he could sleep inside on his seat. This made Albert feel happy to help and the Woodpecker happy to have a place to sleep.

Then one day a small boy came along and he saw Albert. He liked Albert right away. He asked Albert if they could be friends. So he and Albert became friends. They had so much fun together that Albert forgot about his paint. Then one day the little boy came with a big can of car paint. He asked Albert if it would be okay to paint him. Albert was delighted to be painted. The boy sanded and painted with special metal paint. Then he asked Albert to choose a color of paint for the final coat. Albert thought and thought, he liked blue like his friend the blue bird, he liked green like the grass, he liked yellow like the sunshine, and he liked black, white and red like the Woodpecker. He just could not decide.

What color do you think he picked? What do you think happened in the rest of the story? Children will discuss the questions at the end of the story and talk about feelings that Albert the Auto had and that they might have.

Teacher will cut out pictures of different types of boats, cars, trucks, trains, and airplanes. Children will take turns putting the pictures into the three different subcategories of air, water, and ground. They will also tell the names of the pictures and how they help us.

Teacher will prepare bingo cards using different pictures of various transportation in the squares of the bingo card. Teacher will use same pictures as those on the cards to draw and show children. Children will name and look for that form of transportation on their card. They will put a marker on the picture that matches. The play will continue until all the squares are covered. Markers can be buttons, frosty ohs, or any small object.

Prepare four or five small boxes by cutting out a large door in one to make a pretend garage. You will also use four or five small cars. Then tell the children to drive their car into the garage. Next the children will dive their car out of the garage. Then have them drive their car around the garage and fly over the garage. Other positional words can be used like in front, in back, next to, etc. After they are familiar with the positional words have the children tale turns telling the others where to drive their cars.

FREE TIME

CREATIVE ARTS

The easel will be set up with markers and train stamps and stamping pads. Children can draw track, train truss, etc. They can also if they choose to stamp engine and cars on their papers.

SENSORY

Put sand into the table or in the pails with lots of small cars and trucks. Plastic trees could be added along with mountains. Plastic pieces can often be found in the plastic animal toys in the dollar store. Or you can use a floor mat made for cars and trucks for the children to drive the cars around on. You can purchase these or make one with cloth and permanent markers. You could include houses, stores, parks, McDonalds, etc.

DRAMATIC PLAY & SOCIAL DEVELOPMENT

Set up the area with small chairs placed one behind the other. This is the train. Add paper tickets to center along with a paper punch and railroad hats. Dress up clothing and dolls add to this area along with trays and plastic food for the train riders to eat. This allows the children to play "train" and take turns exploring the different roles while having fun.

SCIENCE

Have a pail of water at the science table with various things to find out if they float or sink. Items could be cars, feathers, buttons, wheels, plastic spoons, cotton balls, Popsicle sticks, small airplanes and small plastic people.

GROSS MOTOR

Outside have large boxes with rope straps attached for each arm and the top and bottom of the boxes cut out. Let the children paint them to make cars or buses from them. Also have foam plates for steering wheels and car wheels. Help them attach the wheels with wire. When they are dry children their head through the hole and put the straps over their shoulders and drive around. Put stop signs and speed limit signs up too. If you can get a tall thin box they can make it into a gas plump with the addition of a cut-off piece of garden hose.

FIELD TRIP IDEAS

You could make arrangement for extra parents to go with you on the public bus. It would be nice to take it to a park so the children could play. Take a snack with you for the children. If possible, have one of the helpers meet you there and have them bring the snack along with baby wipes to clean hands and a first aid kit with a change of clothes that would work for either a boy or girl just in case they are needed.

Teacher Resources

LIBRARY BOOKS & MUSIC BY TITLE

The Airplane Book by Edith Kunhardt, Western Publishing Company, Inc., 1987.

Artie the Octagon by John Given, Macmillan Book Clubs, Inc. 1989.

Big Bird's Square Meal, by Emily Thompson,Western Publishing Company, Inc., 1988.

Brown Bear,Brown Bear, What Do You See by Bill Martin Jr./Eric Carle, Henry Holt & Company,1992.

Cars! Cars! Cars! By Grace Maccarone, Scholastic Inc., 2000.

Cat's Colors by Jane Cabrera, Scholastic Inc.,1998.

Circle in Piggyback Songs Warren Publishing House, 1983.

Color Hoedown by Marilyn LaPenta, Macmillan Book Clubs ,Inc.,1989.

The Color Kittens by Margaret Wise Brown, Western Publishing Company, Inc.,1994.

"Down By the Station" and "Sailing At High Tide", Eye Winker Tom Tinker Chin Chopper by Tom Glazer, Doubleday & Company, 1973.

Freight Train by Donald Crews, Published by Scholastics Inc., 1989.

Going Places Western Publishing Company, Inc., 1988.

Huddly Goes to School, by Tedd Arnold Scholastic Inc., 2000.

I've Been Working on the Railroad Nadine Bernard Westcott, Published by Scholastics Inc.,1997.

The Kissing Hand, by Audrey Penn, Scholastic Inc., 1993.

The Little Engine That Could retold by Watty Piper, Price/Stern/Sloan Publishers, Inc., 1986.

My Favorite Color by Heather Forest, Macmillan Book Clubs ,Inc.,1989.

My Many Colored Days by Dr. Seuss, Scholastic Inc.,1997.

My Crayons Talk by Patricia Hubbard, Scholastic Inc.,1997.

One Blue Square in Piggyback Songs Warren Publishing House, 1983.

"Row, Row, Row" from "Raffi Rise and Shine", Homeland Publishing, Rounder Records Corp. Tape & CD.

Sail Away by Donald Crews, Published by Scholastic Inc., 1995.

Seven Blind Mice by Ed Young, Scholastic Inc., 1992.

There's a Square by Mary Sterfoz, Scholastic Inc., 1996.

Truck Talk by Bobbi Katz Published by Scholastic Inc., 1997.

"Wheels on the Bus" from "Raffi Rise and Shine", Homeland Publishing, Rounder Records Corp. Tape & CD.

WHERE TO GET WHAT YOU NEED

There are many different places to get what you need. If you use your imagination, many items can be substituted for what you have on hand, can get for free, etc. For example, you may have an abundance of baby food jars from a family toddler. You can easily convert these to be part of a project. Teaching is also about being resourceful. Have family, friends, students and yourself save:

- Baby food jars

- Toilet paper rolls

- Paper towel rolls

- Scraps of material

- Extra tile

- Extra pieces from home improvement projects

- Coffee cans

- Oatmeal containers

- 2 liter bottles

- cereal boxes

- egg carton

- milk jugs

- salt containers

- anything you can think of to be repurposed for a learning tool

Other places to get materials include:

- Home improvement stores (Lowes or Home Depot)

- Dollar Stores

- Educational Supply Stores

- Grocery Store

- Party Supply Store

- Online Resources:

  o Oriental Trading Company www.orientaltrading.com

  o http://www.etacuisenaire.com

Bonus Material Table of Contents

Fun Recipes For Class

SLIME

1. Combine one cup of water and 1 tsp of borax

2. Fill a plastic cup with about 1/2 inch of glue

3. Add about three tablespoons of water and stir

4. Add three drops of food coloring and stir again

5. Add two tablespoons from the Borax solution and stir well into the glue

6. Lift out the slime and place it on a Ziploc bag

7. Let it sit for 60 seconds then the play can begin.

EATABLE DOUGH

1. Use your favorite sugar cookie recipe and make dough. Allow the children to play with and shape the dough. Make sure you use egg substitute so they can eat their final project.

PLAY DOUGH

1 cup flour

½ cup of salt

¾ cup water

½ tbs oil

1 tsp Cream of Tartar

Food Coloring

Combine above ingredients by hand or in mixer. When completely mixed, dough is ready. This can also be baked and used for crafts, i.e., Christmas Ornaments, etc.

FACE PAINT

1 tsp corn starch

1/2 tsp water

1/2 tsp cold cream

1 drop food coloring

Combine the above ingredients by hand. Use paint brushes to paint on children's faces.

FINGER PAINT

1 cup flour

4 cups water

4 colors of food coloring

Combine flour and 1 cup water into a large saucepan. Stir in water until the mixture is smooth. Add three more cups of water and the turn the heat to medium. Take the mixture to a boil for 75 seconds. Cool the pan on a different burner. Pour into four separate cups and add food coloring as desired. Store in an airtight container.

BUBBLES

1 cup water

¼ cup dish soap

Combine above ingredients in plastic container. Add more soap if desired.

Emergency Contact Information

I/We make every effort to provide a safe and secure environment for your child during class. In order to better to protect the safety and health of your child, I/we request that you provide the following information:

In case of an emergency, I/We will contact the parent listed above. I/We request that the parent provide another contact (not living at the same address) who is authorized by the parent to act on his/her behalf should the parent not be available.

Emergency contact:

Name: _____

Address:_____

Phone Number:_____

Relationship to Parent/Student: _____

PLEASE LIST on the back of this form any health conditions, allergies or diet/mental/ physical restrictions that your child may have and medications that he/she may be using to treat this condition. Indicate if the child has your permission to take such medication while attending the event. You may also include the name of the hospital or doctor of your choice and their phone numbers.

Also if you have made arrangements to have a person other than yourself provide transportation to and from class, please indicate the name and phone number of such person here:

_____

_____

_____

_____

Permission Slip

My son/daughter _____ has permission to participate in the field trip to _____ on_____ ___.

During the activity, I can be reached at: Address _____
Phone Number _____ and Cell Phone Number _____. If I cannot be reached in the event of an emergency, the following person is authorized to act in my behalf:

Name and Address

_____

Relation to Participant _____ Phone_____
Additional Notes _____

_____   _____
(Parent's Signature)   (Date)

By signing this form, I declare that I am the legal parent/guardian of the minor child listed above and authorized to grant such permission and hold harmless the teacher, instructor or any other staff people for any incident that may occur on this field trip.

Fun Field Trip Ideas

Each of our lesson plans already includes ideas for field trips based on the theme of the unit that you are on. However, some times you may need extra ideas or want to do a seasonal field trip. These are ideas used by myself and other educators for children. Most of these ideas can be adapted to any age group and have trained employees to help give you the best experience possible.

1. Doctor's Office

2. Horse Ranch

3. Zoo

4. Police Station

5. Fire Station

6. Park

7. Ice Cream Store like Dairy Queen

8. Bakery
(or Bakery section of a grocery store)

9. Bank

10. Post Office

11. Fishery

12. Sod Farm

13. Cave

14. Dairy Farm

15. Dentist's Office

16. Library

17. Herb Farm

18. Hair Salon

19. Candy Factory
(they are more common than you think)

20. Nursery
(not for children but for plants)

21. Pet Store

22. Veterinarian

23. Ghost Town

24. Bowling

25. Ice Skating

26. Roller Skating

27. Sledding

28. Newspaper Office

29. Glass Factory

30. Car Factory

31. Steel Plant

32. Copper Mine

33. Television Station

34. Lake

35. Children's Museum

36. Public Transportation

37. Aquarium

38. Duck Pond

39. Gas Station

40. Ceramics Store (with Kiln)

41. Local Historic Sites

42. City Council Building

43. Mayor's Office

44. Florist

45. Car Wash

46. Petting Zoo

47. Circus

48. Beach

49. Hospital

50. Swimming Pool

Made in the USA
San Bernardino, CA
01 July 2015